UFO

BY
JOHN DUNCAN

ANCIENT UFOS

'In the 30th year, in the 4th month, on the 5th day, by the river Chebar,' wrote the prophet Ezekiel in the Bible, 'I saw something that looked like burning coals of fire'. Ezekiel described how he saw wheels gleaming like a jewel, 'being as it were a wheel within a wheel.' This could be a description of a gyroscope. Ezekiel interpreted his experience as a vision of God. Nowadays, UFOlogists would suggest it was one of the first recorded sightings of an unidentified flying object (UFO).

ALIEN FOOTPRINT

This fossilized hominid footprint from East Africa was made by an ordinary biped, yet the rock is 3.5 million years old! Some UFOlogists claim the print pre-dates *homo erectus* (prehistoric man) and that it was made by a visiting spaceman.

ANCIENT ABDUCTIONS

Celtic legends told of faery beings who stole babies from their cots and replaced them with faery infants. To keep their babies safe, medieval peasants hung a knife over the cradle. Were these 'faeries' alien scientists?

FOOD FOR THOUGHT

'OCCAM'S RAZOR!'

The medieval thinker William Occam made famous a principle which, in today's language, amounts to: 'Don't invent new weird theories when a simple, common sense answer already exists.' Most of the evidence on this page has a perfectly reasonable explanation, without postulating visits by spacemen.

PREHISTORIC RECORDS

These prehistoric rock drawings from Peru seem to include astronauts wearing space helmets. Cave paintings sometimes show discs in the sky, and the Bible tells us that in prehistory 'the sons of God' came down and took human wives. Could these be ancient references to visits by spacemen?

A DESERT MYSTERY

Over 1,000 years ago, in Nazca, Peru, thousands of stones were arranged to make vast lines and huge figures in the desert. The images, including these 'aliens', are clearly visible from the air but are difficult to distinguish while standing beside them. In 1969, the writer Erich von Däniken suggested that 'ancient astronauts' interfered with humankind's technology and genes and thus shaped human history. He claimed that these Nazca lines were made to be seen by alien visitors from their spaceships.

CULTURAL TRACKING

A Bible story tells of the prophet Elijah being carried away by a chariot of fire. In 1897, Americans saw airships, but in the 1950s metal spaceships were seen (see pages 4-5). UFOs seem to appear in whatever form people expect to see them. This may account for the wide diversity of reported sightings.

FAMOUS SIGHTINGS IN HISTORY

c. 1450 BC, EGYPT
Pharaoh Thutmose III sees 'circles of fire' in the sky.

322 BC, LEBANON
Shining silver shields fly over a city besieged by Alexander the Great. They destroy the walls by firing beams of light at the defences.

AD 840, FRANCE
The Archbishop of Lyons stops people killing two creatures who had come to Earth in a 'cloud ship'.

1211, IRELAND
The people of Cloera try to catch creatures whose 'airship' had caught on their church roof.

1271, JAPAN
The execution of a Buddhist monk is called off when a bright object hangs in the sky above the site.

1492
A sailor on Columbus's ship, the Santa Maria, sees a glittering thing in the sky.

1639, BOSTON, USA
Mr James Everell and friends are fishing when a bright light hovers over them and moves their boat upstream.

1752, SWEDEN
Farmers see a large, shining cylinder in the sky 'give birth' to smaller balls of light.

1762, SWITZERLAND
In different towns, two astronomers independently record a 'spindle-shaped' aircraft move across the face of the sun.

1819, MASSACHUSETTS, USA
Professor Rufus Graves sees a fireball crash into the yard of his friend Erastus Dewey. They find wreckage and, inside it, a foul-smelling pulpy substance.

1820, USA
Mormon leader Joseph Smith sees a UFO and talks with its occupants.

1861, CHILE
Peasants see a metal bird with shining eyes and scraping scales.

1868, ENGLAND
Astronomers at the Radcliffe Observatory, Oxford University, track a UFO for 4 minutes.

1887, BANJOS, SPAIN
Villagers found two 'children' in a cave. Their clothes were strange, they spoke no known language and their skin was green.

SIGHTINGS

UFOs undoubtedly exist. What is in doubt is what they are. Every year, over a thousand sightings are reported, many from people who ask to remain anonymous lest they be thought mad. Famous people who have seen UFOs include two American presidents; Jimmy Carter once watched a UFO while he was attending a dinner party; and President Reagan stunned a White House meeting by announcing he had once seen a UFO from the window of his plane. American astronaut Major Gordon Cooper reported seeing a glowing green object on his space flight in 1963 – an object that had also appeared on Australian radar. In 1965, space-walkers Ed White and James McDivitt reported seeing a metallic UFO, with 'arms' sticking out in all directions.

 ## FOOD FOR THOUGHT

In the 1960s, the American Air Force project Blue Book studied 13,000 UFO sightings. It found only about two per cent were really unidentified. Most UFOs are perfectly natural phenomena. Explanations include:
- *Aircraft and satellites.*
- *Weather balloons.*
- *Jupiter (and other planets) - often unusually bright. A visual illusion called autokinesis can make them seem to move in the sky.*
- *Meteors.*
- *Canadian scientists have found a correlation between UFO phenomena and earthquakes. Stress on rocks just before an earthquake can produce strong electrical fields and strange lights.*
- *Vitreous floaters (matter moving inside the eye itself).*
- *Wishful thinking, hysteria, and emotional disturbance.*

Yes, it is less romantic! But even the UFO sightings not yet explained are also likely to be attributable either to natural phenomena that we don't yet fully understand (such as ball lightning) or to military experiments.

ALIEN WARFARE

This woodcut from 1561 records a frightening event in Germany when black and red balls of light seemed to battle together in the sky. Some UFOlogists suggest that perhaps two alien species were warring for control of the Earth.

A UFO OF THE NINETIES

Jeremy Johnson, who took this photograph in England in 1992, thought at first he had missed his chance, because the round white object vanished as soon as he pointed the camera at it.

THE AIRSHIP PHENOMENON

In 1897, many people in America saw shining, cigar-shaped 'airships'. This illustration was drawn for a newspaper at the time. Nobody would believe that they were seeing an actual airship, even though a certain E.J. Pennington said it belonged to him.

TUNGUSKA DISASTER

In 1908, an explosion in Siberia, Russia, flattened trees for miles around. No impact crater or meteor fragments were found, and modern theories of the cause include a comet or a small black hole. Local people, however, described an elliptical fireball that rose up from the ground. They subsequently experienced an illness resembling radiation sickness. UFOlogists suggest the phenomenon was an exploding spaceship.

FOO FIGHTERS

During the Second World War, many British and American pilots reported seeing small shining discs (which they called 'foo fighters') following their planes and causing the engines to short out. One UFOlogist thought these discs were remotely-controlled alien probes. This Second World War photograph clearly shows these mysterious discs in the sky.

The Flying Saucer as I Saw it... by Kenneth Arnold

UFOLOGY IS BORN

Perhaps the most influential sighting of all was made by Kenneth Arnold in the United States. In June 1947, Arnold saw nine V-shaped UFOs. He told a newspaper reporter that they moved at speeds of over 1,600 km/h (1,000 mph), 'like a saucer would if you skipped it across the water.' The newspaper's subsequent report of 'Flying Saucers' captured the public's imagination. *Fate Magazine* was published a year later, the first of many UFO publications.

THE ROSWELL INCIDENT

This artist's reconstruction of the Roswell incident shows a UFO being struck by lightning in the storm of 4 July 1947.

 FOOD FOR THOUGHT

The US government's denial of the presence of an alien spaceship may have a more common-sense explanation. They may have been trying to keep secret the presence of a Japanese 'balloon bomb' left over from World War II, or a top-secret US 'spy-balloon' designed to monitor Russian nuclear capabilities. In 1947, the US Air Force bomber group at Roswell was the world's only nuclear-weaponed strike force, and it is almost certain that the subsequent government secrecy was motivated by fear of espionage.

THE TRUTH IS OUT THERE

On 8 July, local engineer Grady Barnett added to the Roswell mystery when he and a team of archaeologists claimed to have found a crashed disc-shaped UFO and the bodies of four aliens – small, grey humanoids with large heads. The US Air Force quickly removed these, leaving nothing to be seen. Even an investigation by the US Senate in 1994 failed to convince UFO enthusiasts that their government does *not* still have the wreckage of a UFO and the corpses of aliens. The idea of a secret, crashed UFO – and of what we might learn by 'back-engineering' such a machine – is so attractive that it is impossible to eradicate such beliefs.

THE MOST FAMOUS UFO

Roswell Daily Record

RAAF Captures Flying Saucer On Ranch in Roswell Region

On 4 July 1947, there was a lightning storm over the town of Roswell in New Mexico. Sitting in his farmhouse, rancher William 'Mac' Brazel thought he heard an explosion above the sound of the storm. Next day, riding out to check his sheep, Brazel discovered some wreckage 'like nothing made on Earth'. It crumpled like foil but slowly straightened itself out again and was impervious to blows from a sledgehammer. Brazel reported it to the local air base, only to be arrested and held in custody until the wreckage had been retrieved. This was the prelude to one of the best-known and most durable UFO stories.

CAPTURED!

Since the Arnold 'flying saucer' story of June 1947, the US Air Force had recorded almost a thousand UFO sightings from all over the USA, including reports of downed spacecraft. On 8 July 1947, the commander at the Roswell Air Force base told the press that a flying disc had been recovered from a local site. Immediately, according to the *Roswell Daily Record*, the Roswell wreckage became a crashed UFO from which four aliens had been retrieved.

ALIEN AUTOPSY

In 1996, businessman Ray Santilli released film, on authenticated 1947 filmstock, of autopsies being done on the aliens retrieved from the Roswell crash. The film was like a B-class horror movie and the aliens looked nothing like those supposedly found in the Roswell crash. There was even a modern phone clearly visible in the background. Yet UFO enthusiasts were convinced by the 'evidence' of this film. This picture, from the Roswell International UFO Museum, shows a replica of the alien body from the filmed 'autopsy'.

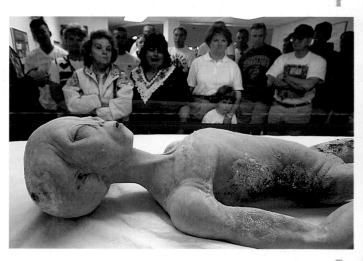

BALLOON WRECKAGE

On the afternoon of 8 July, the US Air Force held two press conferences. A polite, fresh-faced, and very plausible young Warrant Officer showed foil debris from a weather balloon which he said was the cause of the confusion. When asked if it was the remains of a flying saucer, the young man giggled. The explanation was clearly bogus; the government obviously wanted to cover something up. That same month, there were a number of US Air Force cargo flights from Roswell to the top-secret Wright-Patterson Air Force base in Ohio. What they were carrying has never been satisfactorily explained.

FOOD FOR THOUGHT

After four years, the Hessdalen investigators concluded that the lights were probably a natural phenomenon. There is so much about our world that we do not understand, it is highly likely that UFO incidents are, in fact, natural but rare phenomena which we cannot yet explain. Only when we understand everything about our own world will we be able to say that inexplicable events may have been caused by aliens.

CLOSE ENCOUNTERS

During the 1950s and 1960s, there were thousands of UFO sightings but it was not until 1972 that a way of analysing and categorizing them was developed by J. Allen Hynek, a respected UFOlogist. In his book *The UFO Experience*, Dr Hynek was the first UFOlogist to divide the different kinds of UFO event into types of close encounters. Ever since then, UFOlogists have classified UFO events according to his categories, from close encounters of the first kind, to close encounters of the fifth kind. Many UFOlogists also give reports of encounters a *strangeness rating* according to how typical of such events they are.

HESSDALEN LIGHTS

As well as photographing the lights, the researchers used radar, seismographs, infrared viewers, spectrum analysers and Geiger counters, to see if the lights were leaving any physical evidence of their presence.

A CE2: PROJECT HESSDALEN, NORWAY

During 1981-85, Norwegian scientists studied lights that appeared over Hessdalen. The lights moved and seemed to respond to the actions of the observers.

CLOSE ENCOUNTERS OF THE THIRD KIND

Steven Spielberg's 1977 film was based on UFO-logist J. Allen Hynek's book, *The UFO Experience* (1972). In the story, a series of UFO encounters gradually build up to a friendly meeting between aliens and humans (a CE5). It has been suggested that the US government asked Steven Spielberg to make the film to allay public fears about UFOs.

A CE1: THE LUBBOCK LIGHTS, USA

In 1951, the people of Lubbock, Texas, reported a V-shaped formation of lights passing overhead at night. The lights were said to be travelling at about 650 km/h (400 mph).

A nearby radar station also recorded an 'unknown' object. Official explanations of the phenomenon include a flight of geese illuminated by street lights, and an experimental jet bomber being tested in the area.

CATTLE MUTILATIONS, CROP CIRCLES & OTHER CE2s

CROP CIRCLES

In the 1980s, crop circles began to appear all over the world, especially in Britain and, as this example shows, in Japan. UFOlogists suggested they were made by landing spacecraft. Given celebrity status by the newspapers, the circles received a great deal of publicity.

A close encounter of the second kind is when a UFO leaves some physical evidence of its presence. In one famous example, a French farmer from Trans-en-Provence reported in 1981 that an object had landed in his garden. Government investigators found the soil had been heated to 600°C (1,112°F). One scientist suggested the effects had been produced by a strong electro-magnetic field. The story is similar to that of another farmer, M. Masse, who in 1965 claimed that a spaceship had landed in his lavender-field in Valensole – about 48 km (30 miles) from Trans-en-Provence.

A CE2 OF A DIFFERENT KIND

Stephen Michalak, an amateur geologist, claims to have seen a spaceship near Winnipeg, Canada, in 1967. Apparently, when the craft flew away the heat was so intense that his clothes were set on fire. Later, the pattern of a grille appeared burned on to Michalak's chest. Some sceptics claimed that Michalak had burned himself but scientists found evidence of radioactivity and extreme heat at the landing site.

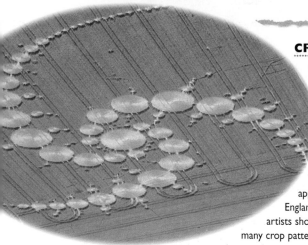

CROP ART

One Australian suggested crop circles were caused by courting coots. A British expert blamed stampeding hedgehogs. But when a meteorologist said they were caused by stationary tornadoes, elaborate crop patterns started to appear which could not possibly have been made by the weather. This beautiful example appeared in Wiltshire, England. In 1991, two retired artists showed how they had faked many crop patterns in Britain. Strangely, many hoaxers have reported seeing UFOs while they were working on the crop patterns.

 FOOD FOR THOUGHT

Why would aliens fly 2,000 light-years to fiddle about in fields, and why would such technologically sophisticated beings need thousands of animal organs for their studies? These stories are so unbelievable that no one should ever think they are the work of alien visitors. The real danger is that, swamped by the thousands of hoaxers and cranks, our scientists may miss the one witness who has had a genuine CE2!

HOW DID SNIPPY DIE?

In 1967, a horse called *Snippy* (or *Lady* in some accounts) was found dead on a ranch in Colorado. Her head had been skinned with a straight cut and her internal organs had been removed. There was no blood on the ground, and there were circular exhaust-marks all around the body. Similar cases have been reported from all over the world, notably a large number of horse mutilations in England in the 1980s.

CATTLE MUTILATION

There have been hundreds of reports of mutilations of cattle, such as this example from New Mexico, USA. Some people suggest they are the work of Satanists, but investigations of individual animals have shown that the blood in the flesh on either side of the cuts has been cooked at a temperature of about 150°C (302°F), yet the cells around the incisions remained undamaged. Today, we know of no instruments capable of doing this.

Aboard a Flying Saucer

by TRUMAN BETHURUM

Non-Fiction—A True Account of Factual Experience

TRUMAN BETHURUM
CONTACTEE, 1954

Bethurum was a road-layer who in 1954 claimed to have met aliens in the California desert near Las Vegas. His visitors had olive green skin and dark hair. They came from Clarion, a planet obscured from the Earth by the moon. Clarion, Bethurum was told, had no disease, crime, nor politicians.

ABOARD A
FLYING SAUCER

Bethurum claimed he had actually been taken aboard the alien spaceship where he met the craft's captain, a beautiful alien called Aura Rhanes who spoke in rhyme. Bethurum met her romantically a number of times, much to the annoyance of his wife! Bethurum wrote a successful book about his experiences.

Flyin Hav

Desm Ge

 FOOD FOR THOUGHT

All this evidence, like all UFO evidence, is merely anecdotal. It confirms UFOlogy as no more than a pseudo-science, based on unsubstantiated stories and hearsay. The stories are obviously ridiculous. Today, our interest in them is not whether they are true but why so many people in the 1950s were so easily taken in by these sad deceptions, and what has changed in our society to make us less likely to believe such stories.

AN ALIEN IN NEW JERSEY, 1957

Born in 1922, Howard Menger says he first saw 'space-people' as a child and also had many close encounters while in the army. In his book *From Outer Space to You* (1959), he wrote about meeting Venusians, some over 500 years old. They included a number of beautiful women in transparent ski-suits – although the spacewoman in this photograph seems to be wearing a more conventional spacesuit. Menger claims to have helped the Venusians fit into Earthly society, cutting the men's long hair and offering the women bras! Menger said his second wife Marla was from Venus. In the 1960s, Menger claimed the Central Intelligence Agency (CIA) had asked him to make up the encounters so that they could test public reaction to UFO stories. He also claims men in black (see page 20) tried to prevent him talking about his sightings.

(see page 20)

TAKE ME TO YOUR LEADER!

In a close encounter of the fifth kind there is interaction between aliens and humans. The great age of the *contactee* was the 1950s, when many books were published on the subject and meetings with space beings were described by a number of speakers at public lectures. Nowadays, UFOlogists are embarrassed by these stories which tend to discredit genuine UFO research.

JOE SIMONTON, USA

Many other people claimed to have met space visitors. One strange case was that of sixty-year-old chicken farmer Joe Simonton of Wisconsin. In 1961, he was visited by small, dark-skinned spacemen wearing black suits and knitted balaclavas! The aliens asked him for a jug of water, and in return gave him some pancakes. Simonton ate one of the pancakes, which tasted like cardboard, and sent the others for analysis. They were made out of ordinary flour but with no salt. Local people said Simonton was a quiet, ordinary man who did not make up amazing stories.

FLYING SAUCERS HAVE LANDED

George Adamski was a burger-bar waiter who later gave himself the title of 'Professor'. He had written a novel about meeting a man from Venus but hadn't found a publisher. When he re-modelled his story as fact, his book *Flying Saucers Have Landed* (1953) became a bestseller.

Leslie & Adamski

GEORGE ADAMSKI
CONTACTEE, 1953

In 1953, after seeing a UFO in the California desert, Adamski went to investigate. He met a handsome, sun-tanned young Venusian with long, sandy-coloured hair who told him – using hand signs and telepathy – that Venus was Earth's sister planet. The Venusians had come to warn humanity that nuclear radiation could ruin the Earth. Adamski later claimed to have been taken by his Venusian friends to Mars, Saturn and Jupiter.

FOOD FOR THOUGHT

One in six people need psychiatric help at some time in their adult life. 'Abduction' experiences are probably a form of mental delusion. The Hills and the Walton cases (see pages 16-17) both illustrate the power of television to influence our subconscious minds. Even under hypnosis it is possible to tell lies, and there is considerable evidence that hypnotists can 'suggest' UFO ideas to an abductee. Indeed, experiments have been done in which subjects were able to invent realistic 'imaginary abductions' under hypnosis. People have been observed having an abduction experience. In one case in Australia, two people watched as someone (who never left their sight) apparently 'met' aliens and 'went into' a spaceship. It was clearly a real event inside the head of the 'abductee' but all the two witnesses saw was the abductee's physical responses to what he seemed to be experiencing. Most abduction 'memories' are similar. They involve tunnels, lights, being covered in liquid, finding it hard to breathe, pain in the navel, being medically examined, etc. Women abductees remember having eggs taken from their ovaries, or even being implanted with alien foetuses. In these details, most 'abductions' seem more like a flashback to the experience of being born rather than of an alien encounter.

ABDUCTION CASEBOOK

In the **USA**, a recent survey suggested one in twenty people believe they have been abducted. One **UFO**logist claims we have all been abducted at one time or another! Many victims only realize they have been abducted after their memories are drawn out by regression therapy (by which a hypnotist takes them back to re-live events in their past). A phenomenon which involves so many people is certainly worth investigation.

ALL OF THE FOLLOWING SYMPTOMS HAVE BEEN CONSIDERED EVIDENCE OF AN ABDUCTION

- 'Lost' time, which cannot be accounted for.
- Scars, bruises or burns with no memory of what caused them.
- Nightmares, especially about aliens, flying, or being eaten by animals with large eyes (such as owls).
- Insomnia, especially when caused by fear of going sleep.
- Medical problems, such as vomiting, headaches, tiredness, or rashes.
- Depression.
- A UFO sighting; experience of *déjà vu*; or a feeling of having 'second sight', the ability to foresee the future or see events happening elsewhere.
- An image repeatedly comes to mind (perhaps put in the brain to block memory).
- Unaccountable black marks on an X-ray.

IMPLANTS

Some UFOlogists believe aliens implant tracking devices in the people they abduct so that they can locate them later. This implant was found in the roof of an abductee's mouth. Above, 17-year-old abductee James Basel with his alleged alien implant.

CASE STUDY 1: ANTONIO VILLAS BOAS, BRAZIL

Name/Occupation: Antonio Villas Boas. Farmer.
Date: Approx. 16 October 1957.
Location: Francisco de Sales, Brazil.

Case Description: The day after seeing a UFO, Villas Boas was alone on his tractor, ploughing a field. Dragged on board an egg-shaped craft by three humanoids, he was stripped, covered in a clear liquid, and had a blood sample taken from his chin. Later, a beautiful naked humanoid came in and had sex with him.

Investigator's Notes: Villas Boas tried to fight off his abductors. Doctors found marks and scars all over his body. He suffered sickness and sleepiness which resembled radiation poisoning. Villas Boas remembered his experience without regression therapy and never changed his story. Boas remembered seeing some writing over the door of the UFO craft.

An artist's impression of Antonio's abductor and the alien craft that landed in his field.

CASE STUDY 2: BETTY AND BARNEY HILL, USA

Name/Occupation: Betty (retired social worker) and Barney Hill.
Date: 19 September 1961.
Location: New Hampshire, USA.

Case Description: On their way home one evening, Betty and Barney were frightened by a UFO. They later found marks on their bodies and realized they had 'lost' two hours. Nightmares and depression followed. Under regression hypnosis they remembered being abducted by creatures with 'wrap-around' eyes. Barney had been forced to give a sperm sample. A needle had been inserted into Betty's navel.

Betty remembered a 'star map' the aliens had shown her and drew a copy of it. From this, UFOlogists deduced the aliens came from Zeta Reticuli, about 30 light years from Earth.

Investigator's Notes: Although the Hills are often described as an 'ordinary couple', Betty has had many psychic experiences. At one time, she claimed UFOs followed her everywhere. Her psychiatrist believed she was suffering delusions after a frightening experience and that her husband had adopted her anxieties into his own memory. Their abduction happened shortly after a sci-fi programme on TV had depicted aliens with 'wrap-around' eyes.

An artist's impression of Betty and Barney during their encounter with a UFO.

CASE STUDY 3: TRAVIS WALTON, USA

Name/Occupation: Travis Walton. Forester.
Date: 5 November 1975.
Location: Arizona, USA.

Case Description: One night in November 1975, the seven men of a logging team saw a UFO. When Walton went to investigate he was paralysed by a beam of light from the craft. His friends fled, leaving him for dead. Five days later, Walton turned up in a nearby town. Under regression hypnosis he remembered a typical abduction. He was examined by three tall aliens with large eyes, and was shown a hangar full of UFOs.

Investigator's Notes: The Hills's abduction story had appeared on TV only a month before this incident. The team were behind on their logging contract and wanted an excuse. Travis Walton was known as a practical joker. But, 25 years later, not one of the seven-man team has changed his story.

Travis Walton wrote a book. His experience was made into a film, Fire in the Sky, in which some of the facts were changed. Nonetheless, the team made a lot of money from their story.

CASE STUDY 4: LINDA NAPOLITANO, USA

Name/Occupation: Linda Napolitano. Housewife.
Date: 30 November 1989.
Location: New York, USA.

Case Description: In 1989, Linda Napolitano was having hypnosis therapy because she believed she had been abducted a number of times. During her treatment, she revealed she had been abducted again. Under hypnosis, Linda remembered being taken out through the walls of her 12th-storey apartment into a spaceship high above the streets of Manhattan. She was medically examined, then returned to her bed.

Investigator's Notes: In 1991, this amazing story was given credence when two Manhattan police officers, who later claimed to be secret service men, reported that they had seen a woman floating in the sky and being taken into a UFO. Later, another witness also claimed to have seen the event.

An artist's impression of Linda Napolitana's abduction from her Manhattan apartment

FAKES

UFOlogy is a tempting field for con-men who want to make money, and publicity-seekers who want to be famous. Some of the best work to expose fakes is done by responsible UFOlogists who know that fraudulent claims only add to public and government scepticism. The pictures on these pages show how some of the people can be fooled some of the time.

ROSWELL REVISITED

This effect, taken at Roswell, USA, was achieved by photographing a UFO-like object thrown towards the setting sun.

VENUSIAN SCOUT CRAFT

Effects (FX) technology has improved so much that some past fakes now look ridiculous. This photograph of a 'scout craft' taken by George Adamski (see page 13) looks no more sophisticated than a metal lampshade and some light bulbs. What Venusian would be brave enough to set off across the solar system in one of these?

 FOOD FOR THOUGHT

UFO photographers can't win, can they? Blurred blobs are rejected as too indistinct to show anything; brilliant images are dismissed as too good to be true. Nevertheless, after a century of UFO interest in the camera age, there is not one, unquestioned, clear photograph of a UFO.

STRANGE CLOUDS, HAWAII

Photographed near Hawaii, this UFO is, in fact, a lenticular cloud formation, lit by the rays of the setting sun.

UFOs OVER NEW YORK

Modern FX technology makes it harder to distinguish the fake from the real. What is suspicious about this shot of UFOs over New York?

ALPINE FAKE, ITALY

This UFO in the Bernina Mountains is probably a table-top model, photographed close up. The spacesuited alien is almost certainly a toy soldier. It was exposed as a fake by the Italian Ufologico Nationale.

HOW TO DETECT A FAKE PHOTOGRAPH

- *Lack of adequate perspective reference that would indicate the size and position of an object, suggests that the UFO is a model that has been hung up or thrown.*
- *Variations in the grain of a photo indicate an image has been 'pasted' into it.*
- *Irregularities in the angles of light (and shadows) between the object and the background are evidence of separate images pasted together.*
- *Differences in colour, clarity, or brightness between the UFO and the rest of the photo are often a sign that the UFO has been painted or stuck on to a pane of glass in front of the camera.*
- *Bright luminous blobs or streaks may be blemishes on the film negative, or lens flare and reflection. These account for many UFO pictures caught by accident.*
- *Such things as tree branches or telephone lines above a UFO indicate that an object might have been hung up close to the camera.*
- *Photographs conveniently blurred, fuzzy, or indistinct, suggest a model which the photographer has tried to disguise.*

AREA 51, USA

According to the US government, Area 51 in Nevada does *not* exist – the area is blank on the map. In fact, it is a *secret* US air base that may be used for testing prototype military aircraft, such as unmanned aerial vehicles (above right), or for dumping waste from nuclear weapons. UFO-watchers regularly see craft performing aerial manoeuvres there at night. They believe Area 51 is where the US government has stored the Roswell UFO (see pages 6-7).

A SECRET TECHNOLOGY

According to Bob Lazar, the US Government has recovered some crashed UFOs and is 'back-engineering' their technology to see how they work.

MEN IN BLACK (MIB)

UFO witnesses have sometimes been followed by 'men in black' who look like agents of the Federal Bureau of Investigation (FBI). Some UFO-believers claim the MIB are aliens trying to suppress the truth. Or perhaps they *are* FBI agents. This MIB is from the Hollywood film of the same name.

AREA 51:CONSPIRACY

'**D**on't be fooled!' say **UFO** enthusiasts. 'Aliens do exist. The government knows about them and has worked with them for many years. But there is a cover-up to stop you getting to know.' To be a **UFO**-believer, it is almost necessary to be a conspiracy-believer. Conspiracy theories are immune to contradiction because they are beyond proof or disproof. No matter what a government does or says, the conspiracy-believer shouts, 'trick'. Even when a claim is proved to be ridiculous or a hoax, conspiracy-believers simply assert that they have been misinformed by the government in order to discredit them.

BOB LAZAR

According to Bob Lazar, who claims he once worked at Area 51, the US government has nine UFOs stored there. Although there is no evidence that Lazar ever worked at Area 51, nor of his gaining an Engineering degree from the university he claims to have attended, his testimony is often taken as proof that there is a conspiracy to cover up the truth!

MAJESTIC 12

In 1984, a TV company was sent some documents on photographic film. They seemed to prove that a group of experts called the Majestic 12 had been set up in 1947 to study the Roswell UFO. The fact that the documents had been typed on a typewriter not invented until 1963 was ignored, and conspiracy-believers still think they prove the US government has a UFO. They say if the documents were faked, they were faked by the government in a conscious attempt at disinformation!

TOP SECRET
EYES ONLY
THE WHITE HOUSE
WASHINGTON

September 24, 1947.

MEMORANDUM FOR THE SECRETARY OF DEFENSE

Dear Secretary Forrestal,

As per our recent conversation on this matter, you are hereby authorized to proceed with all due speed and caution upon your undertaking. Hereafter this matter shall be referred to only as Operation Majestic Twelve.

It continues to be my feeling that any future considerations relative to the ultimate disposition of this matter should rest solely with the Office of the President following appropriate discussions with yourself, Dr. Bush and the Director of Central Intelligence.

TOP SECRET
EYES ONLY

FOOD FOR THOUGHT

The American psychologist Elaine Showalter believes conspiracy theories are deeply damaging to society because they poison our faith in our institutions. We used to believe we could always ask a policeman for help. Now, we feel that no matter who we elect no government official or department can be trusted. Conspiracy-believers have made the world a frightening and lonely place.

IS ANYBODY OUT THERE?

The universe is infinite. Even if life on Earth was created by chance, the universe is so big that somewhere in the vast expanse of space the circumstances that led to life on Earth could also have occurred elsewhere. Surely infinite space cannot be devoid of other life forms? Well, so argue science fiction buffs and many UFOlogists. Out there, they say (as any *Star Trek* fan knows), there are hundreds of different races of every possible shape, size and colour. Or are there?

MARS FACE

The Viking expedition to Mars in 1976 photographed a rock formation, 3 km (2 miles) long, that looked like a face. Nearby was a collection of pyramid-shaped rocks. UFOlogists claimed it was an ancient Egyptian-like civilization on the shores of a Martian sea. But in 1998, when Mars Global Surveyor re-photographed the area from a different angle, the 'Mars Face' looked like a meteor-battered mountain – exactly what it had always been.

BEYOND OUR DREAMS

Since the nearest star to Earth is 24,000,000,000,000 miles away, SETI thinks it is 'unlikely' aliens have visited our planet. It prefers to see UFOs as 'paranormal' phenomena. Even so, UFOlogists still find it hard to believe that, in the infinite vastness of space, there is not life out there somewhere.

SETI

The Search for Extra-terrestrial Intelligence (SETI) began on 8 April 1960. SETI radio telescopes at the huge Aricebo Observatory in Puerto Rico search for radio signals from the stars. On the first day, a regular 'whoop, whoop' was detected from a star named Epsilon Eridani. Since then, nothing.

LIFE ON MARS

In Antarctica in 1984, a meteorite was discovered that matched the Martian rock studied by the 1976 Mars Viking expedition. Scientists found organic molecules and tiny possible fossils. The excitement is not that life exists on Mars, but that life can develop on other planets.

EXTRASOLAR PLANETS

This is an artist's impression, but astronomers really have discovered planets in outer space. They use the displacements of a star's spectrum (the 'doppler shift') to detect 'wobbles' in its spinning. These betray the existence of another body in orbit around it. In October 1997, astronomers at a Swiss observatory discovered a planet circling the star 51 Pegasi. It is half the size of Jupiter, orbits just 7 million km (4,350,000 miles) from its star in a 'year' of only four days, and has a surface temperature of perhaps 1,300°C (2,372°F).

FOOD FOR THOUGHT

In November 1961, the American radio astronomer Frank Drake (who later became president of the SETI Institute) gave the lecture which changed our thinking about 'Is there life in space?'. The answer, he said, is a mathematical equation:

$$N = R^* \times f_p \times n_e \times f_l \times f_i \times f_c \times L$$

He explained that the number (N) of 'space' civilizations is equal to the number of Earth-type stars in the Milky Way (R^*), times the fraction of stars with planets (f_p), times the number of those planets capable of supporting life (n_e), times the fraction of planets on which life does, by chance, occur (f_l), and evolves intelligence (f_i), and develops an advanced scientific civilization like ours (f_c), times the number of years that the civilization survives (L). The problem with this equation is that we don't know the value of any of the factors in it. However, we can make some reasonable assumptions so that you can do the equation yourself.

1. In the Milky Way there are about 25 billion stars roughly similar to our sun (= R^*).

2. Guess that one in five have planets (so $R^* \times f_p$ = 25 billion x $\frac{1}{5}$).

3. Guess that each of those stars has 2 planets like Earth ($n_e = 2$), that life evolves on one in a hundred ($f_l = \frac{1}{100}$), intelligent life on a tenth of those ($f_i = \frac{1}{10}$), and scientific system comparable to ours on a tenth of those ($f_c = \frac{1}{10}$).

4. Guess that each of those civilizations lasts 1,000 years, in a universe which has existed at least 10,000 million years, so L = a millionth (i.e., divide by a million).

Work it out. How many Earth-like scientific civilizations are there in the Milky Way?

WHAT SHOULD I DO IF I MEET AN ALIEN?

Many UFO enthusiasts believe that aliens are among us. One crank on the Internet claims to have located 136 alien bases on Earth, with 14,619 aliens and a 'robot army' of about 5,000 humans implanted with mind-controlling chips. Science fiction has imagined ever more sinister aliens, in a variety of different forms. The sequence of *Alien* films depict beings impervious to human technology. They have acid for blood, no feelings or morality, and use humans as host incubators. The prospect of humankind ever being visited by such entities is terrifying. So, what kind of alien are you likely to encounter out on the moors on a dark and stormy night?

 FOOD FOR THOUGHT

If you meet an alien, RUN! Modern UFO writers don't claim all aliens are dangerous but there is enough evidence to convince you not to take the risk.
SETI have sent radio messages into space. The 1977 Voyager Space probe carried the message 'Greetings. We step out into the universe seeking only peaceful contact.' They may as well have said, 'Please come and eat us!'
A common feature of abduction reports is that the aliens take small meaningless things from humans. In one story, aliens stole a bunch of flowers from a woman. In another, they took fishing flies and banknotes. So, if you can't run from the aliens, be sure to have some attractive trinket on you. It might distract them while you get away!

CHUPACABRAS (goat-eaters)

This group of aliens are said to live in the caves of Puerto Rico. Measuring a little over 1 metre (3 ft) tall, they have huge red eyes, fangs, long claws, and vampire-wings. They come out at night to mutilate, kill and eat livestock. Some UFOlogists think they are the crew of a crashed spaceship, but they may be creatures that escaped into the jungle when a hurricane destroyed a secret government research installation.

MIDGET MARTIANS

Like these midgets from the film *The Man in the Moon*, aliens may be from a highly developed civilization, be loving and lovable, and will usher in a world of health and happiness!

THE GREYS

Greys are the aliens typical of most abduction stories, about 1.5 metres (4½ ft) tall with large heads and wrap-around eyes. They come from Andromeda or Zeta Reticuli. Their military, totalitarian society aims to conquer Earth and make us their slaves. They have no feelings, and conduct their medical and genetic experiments without anaesthetic.

THE WORLD'S MYSTERIES EXPLORED

FATE

JANUARY 1978 75¢

DEATH BY
HELL'S FIRE

CLOSE ENCOUNTERS OF THE THIRD KIND

REPORT A UFO AT YOUR OWN RISK

. . .Plus Many Other
Intriguing Features

GREEN-SKINNED MONSTERS

Reports say that UFOs can 'turn off' human technology and shoot down military planes. They have paralysing beams and can abduct whole regiments of men. They do nasty experiments on people. If they exist, these beings are far more advanced than us, and they are dangerous!

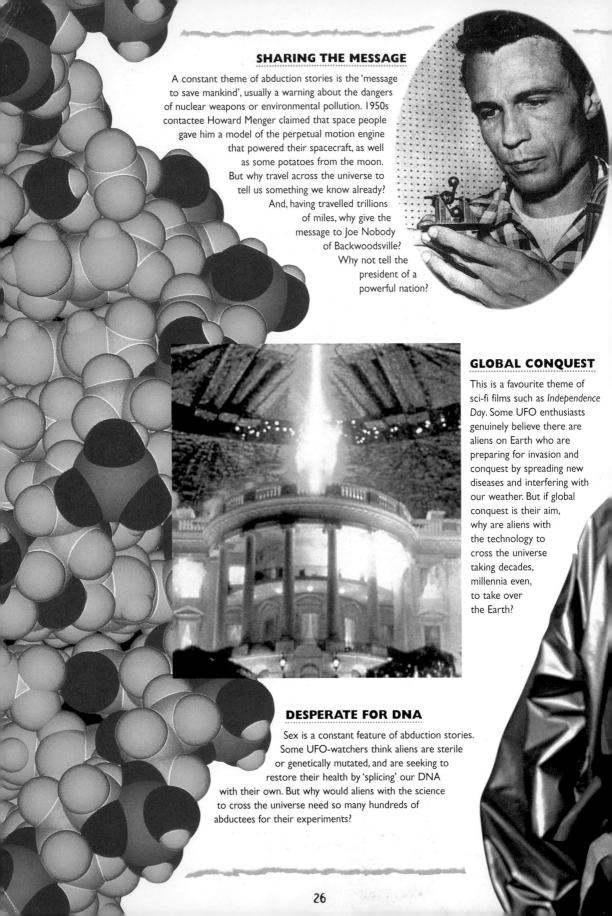

SHARING THE MESSAGE

A constant theme of abduction stories is the 'message to save mankind', usually a warning about the dangers of nuclear weapons or environmental pollution. 1950s contactee Howard Menger claimed that space people gave him a model of the perpetual motion engine that powered their spacecraft, as well as some potatoes from the moon. But why travel across the universe to tell us something we know already? And, having travelled trillions of miles, why give the message to Joe Nobody of Backwoodsville? Why not tell the president of a powerful nation?

GLOBAL CONQUEST

This is a favourite theme of sci-fi films such as *Independence Day*. Some UFO enthusiasts genuinely believe there are aliens on Earth who are preparing for invasion and conquest by spreading new diseases and interfering with our weather. But if global conquest is their aim, why are aliens with the technology to cross the universe taking decades, millennia even, to take over the Earth?

DESPERATE FOR DNA

Sex is a constant feature of abduction stories. Some UFO-watchers think aliens are sterile or genetically mutated, and are seeking to restore their health by 'splicing' our DNA with their own. But why would aliens with the science to cross the universe need so many hundreds of abductees for their experiments?

WHY ARE THEY HERE?

The main flaw in all accounts of alien visitors is how they got here. One respected **UFO**logist thinks there are alien civilizations in the galaxy but the nearest is 2,000 light years away. Travelling at the speed of light sounds feasible in science fiction. In reality, the technology to 'fold space' or to reconstitute at its destination a being who has been 'transported' seems impossible. For travellers at the speed of light, time comes to a standstill. In the time it takes to think, 'I must stop now,' they would travel an infinite distance in (for the rest of us) an infinite amount of time. They would end up beyond the universe at a time when everyone and everything was long since dead. And, given the difficulty of getting here, *why should aliens want to visit the Earth?* What have we got that they could possibly want? Until we meet one who can tell us, theories abound! Some of them are shown on these pages.

SCIENTIFIC EXPERIMENTS

Some UFO enthusiasts believe the human race is a huge genetic experiment. Some think that because aliens have no emotions they want to study concepts such as love, fear, and pain. This cover picture from a 1935 magazine shows that these ideas have a long history.

INTER-GALACTIC TOURISM

The film, *Morons from Outer Space*, in which a group of extra-terrestrial tourists (literally) bump into the Earth, suggests another possible reason. Perhaps the Earth is a galactic wildlife sanctuary run by aliens. Their rangers come to check that the human animals are healthy. Visitors are meant to stay out of sight but sometimes they become over-inquisitive or accidentally knock off the invisibility button. And, of course, there is limited hunting!

 FOOD FOR THOUGHT

The problem with all of these theories is the discrepancy between the sophistication needed to cross the universe to get to Earth, and the lack of progress the aliens make when they get here. Whether they come as scientific human-watchers trying to stay hidden, conquerors trying to overwhelm us, or do-gooders with a message to impart, after 50 years they have all proved singularly incompetent in achieving their aim!

TIME-SLIP

Occasionally, radio-waves
seem to 'wobble' and listeners
find their programme
interrupted briefly by a
completely different channel.
We imagine time as a knife-
edge rushing along with a void
before it and obliteration
behind it. But if time were
like a radio signal that can
sometimes wobble, UFOs
might be a random glimpse
of the future.

Time-slip would also explain
things like sightings of the
Loch Ness monster, of ghosts
and the 'walking dead', and of
disorienting experiences such
as *déjà vu*, in which we have a
sense of something having
happened before.

THEORIES

Some UFOlogists think the popular definition of an alien as an extraterrestrial (ET) is misleading. Today, most UFOlogists accept it is unlikely that Earth is being visited from other galaxies. Instead, they prefer to define alien as 'something outside normal human experience'. Perhaps, some say, aliens are a spiritual manifestation. A 1950s contactee, Richard Miller, claimed an alien from Alpha Centauri told him UFOs were angels. Other people believe UFOs are demons. The founder of the Aetherius Society, George King (a London taxi driver recruited by aliens in 1954 to help save the world from an intelligent meteor) claimed Jesus Christ was an alien from Venus. Other UFOlogists assert that UFO experiences are a real phenomenon but seek explanations which do not involve little green men in spaceships.

ANOTHER DIMENSION

UFO experiences may be the result of our three-dimensional world co-existing with other worlds that have more or fewer dimensions. A creature living in a two-dimensional world would have no height, only length and breadth (like a sheet of paper). Such a creature would not be able to see up or down, as 'up' and 'down' would not exist in its two-dimensional world. It would only be aware of a very thin slice of the universe.

Now imagine if a ball were to pass through this creature's world. Until the ball broke through, the creature would be unaware of it altogether. Then it would see a mysterious circular shape appearing, growing in diameter, then getting smaller again and finally disappearing as the ball finished passing through. If Earth shares space with and occasionally overlaps other-dimensional worlds, then glimpses of these would be just as fleeting and puzzling for us.

THE 'OZ' FACTOR

Known as the Oz factor, a still and eerie quiet is often reported to occur just prior to an alien encounter. UFOlogist Jenny Randles draws attention to the similarity between UFO events and paranormal phenomena such as extra-sensory perception (ESP), out-of-body, and near-death experiences. She accepts the possibility of other beings in the universe but wonders if they are trying to get in touch on a psychic level.

WAKING DREAMS

These psychological experiences can be so vivid that in the dreamer's memory it may not be clear what was dream and what was reality. Many waking dreams are disorienting, terrifying events. Later, to come to terms with the trauma the brain might assign to it a symbolic but nevertheless concrete and explicable reality. In the past, people blamed ghosts or demons for their hallucinations but, today, because sci-fi images and sophisticated technology are familiar to us, our brain is likely to attribute such experiences to aliens.

 FOOD FOR THOUGHT

These ideas are a retreat from UFOlogy as scientific fact, into UFO-faith – where you can't prove, but simply believe. In that sense, they demonstrate that no one has been able to prove that extraterrestrial spacecraft exist.

WHY ARE WE SO INTERESTED?

In 1960, two French writers, Jacques Bergier and Louis Pauwels, published *The Morning of the Magicians*, a book which argued that science didn't have all the answers. Society, they said, was like a car speeding along a motorway – it was going somewhere all right, but what about the fields and villages on either side? **By heading off down the science/technology road, they suggested, humankind was missing many of the important truths about life. The book revived interest in experiences that couldn't be scientifically explained. Perhaps part of the reason people are so interested in UFOs is that they are, and remain, a mystery, despite the many theories about them.**

ESCAPISM

Prince Gautama Siddhartha (Buddha) lived in a palace and never saw the real world. One day, he went out and was so horrified by the suffering he saw that he left the palace for ever. Today, we see the miseries of the world on television all the time. In a sense, we enjoy 'going back into the palace' – getting away from reality and into a fantasy world.

 FOOD FOR THOUGHT

Interest in UFOs and stories about alien encounters is probably here to stay. We are intrinsically fascinated by the unknown and the frightening. In a world where we are realizing that hating other groups of human beings is wrong, perhaps we need the idea of some external threat such as sinister aliens – if only to play the 'baddies' in the movies! Extraterrestrial UFOs can never be debunked, because science can prove only that something does exist, not that it doesn't.

THE MARTIANS ARE COMING!

In 1938, a radio adaptation of *The War of the Worlds*, a book by H.G. Wells, was so realistic it created panic when broadcast in America. Despite regular announcements that the play was fictional, William Dock, 76, from Grover's Mill, USA (where Martians had supposedly landed) was ready with a shotgun to ward off the imaginary invaders. People seemed almost to want the story to be true!

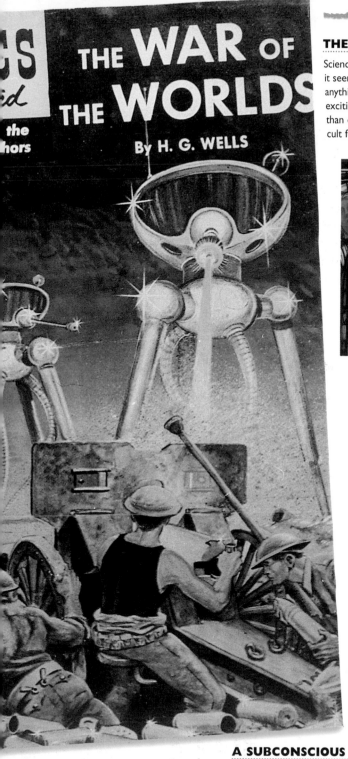

THE WAR OF THE WORLDS

By H. G. WELLS

THE RISE OF SCI-FI

Science-fiction began in the nineteenth century, when it seemed that science would eventually be able to do anything. Readers found it fascinating, frightening, and exciting. Today, interest in science-fiction is stronger than ever, and programmes like *Star-Trek* have huge, cult followings.

THE SEARCH FOR SOMETHING BEYOND OURSELVES

The psychological need for 'something out there' that is bigger than we are is as old as humankind. Today, fewer people go to church but the need for something beyond themselves can lead to a belief in the occult or the paranormal. Interest in UFOs is perhaps part of this. One example is the Aetherius Society (see page 29). Another is the *Urantia Book* which was written in the 1930s by Dr William Sadler, a psychiatrist and theologian. The *Urantia Book* teaches that the universe is full of many beings – gods, angels and mortals (among which are human beings). It is not a religion but people do attend study fellowships about it.

A SUBCONSCIOUS IMAGE

In his 1958 book, *Flying Saucers, a Modern Myth*, the great psychologist Carl Jung called UFOs a 'rumour'. He said UFOs appeal to our subconscious – even their circular shape is a powerful subconscious image – and embody our deepest hopes and fears that science and technology will either save or destroy us. He concluded that to be fascinated by UFOs is a natural and inevitable function of our psychology.

DID YOU KNOW?

After a UFO sighting, delicate cobweb-like strands called 'angel hair' are often found at the site. A false image on a radar screen is also called an 'angel' (or ghost).

Some UFOlogists believe that UFOs are, as yet undiscovered, translucent creatures that live in the sky.

Many abductees report seeing an alien that looks like an intelligent baby and is a hybrid of human and alien genes.

One government study of unexplained aerial phenomena was called 'Project Twinkle'. It had only one camera and failed to photograph a single UFO.

Some people claim they can 'channel' the voices of aliens through their own bodies, a bit like a medium claims to speak on behalf of the dead.

A 'flap' is the publicity surrounding a UFO incident. A 'wave' is a number of sightings from all over the world in quick succession. A 'hot spot' is a place where UFOs are often seen.

Some people claim to be able to visualize events and objects far away by using paranormal powers. Sometimes, they 'see' UFOs over the objects.

The government of the former Soviet Union took UFOs very seriously, and organized a series of investigations. Russia even has its own 'Area-51', an area in the Ural Mountains known as the 'M-zone'.

One UFOlogist claims that UFOs move as they do by generating an electrical and gravitational field to cancel out their own mass. By varying the field strength, they can move up or down at great speeds.

You can find out loads more about UFOs on the Internet. Why not check out these websites?

AUFORA http://ume.med.ucalgary.ca/~watanabe/ufo.html

ARUFON http://user.mc.net/~wdiggs/ufo.htm

BUFORA (The British UFO Research Organisation) http://www.bufora.org.uk

MUFON http://www.rutgers.edu/~mcgrew/mufon/index.html

Robert Sheaffer's The UFO Skeptic's Page http://hugin.imat.com/~sheaffer/ufo.html

Roswell Resource Center http://ds.dial.pipex.com/ritson/scispi/roswell/index.htm

SETI Institute http://www.seti-inst.edu

ACKNOWLEDGEMENTS

We would like to thank: Helen Wire and Elizabeth Wiggans for their assistance.

Copyright © 1999 ticktock Publishing Ltd.

First published in Great Britain by ticktock Publishing Ltd., The Offices in the Square, Hadlow, Tonbridge, Kent TN11 0DD, Great Britain.

All rights reserved.

No part of this publication may be reproduced, stored in a retrieval system, or transmitted in any form or by any means electronic, mechanical, photocopying, recording or otherwise, without prior written permission of the copyright owner.

A CIP catalogue record for this book is available from the British Library. ISBN 1 86007 106 6 (paperback). ISBN 1 86007 142 2 (hardback).

Picture research by Image Select. Printed in Hong Kong.

Picture Credits: t = top, b = bottom, c = centre; l = left, r= right, OFC = outside front cover, OBC = outside back cover, IFC = inside front cover

Alastair Carew-Cox; 31cr. Ann Ronan/Image Select; 3b, 31br. Corbis; 24b & OBC; 20bl. Corbis Royalty Free Images; 14/15 & 32. Fortean Picture Library; 2/3cb, 4b, 4c, 5bl, 6/7b, 7tr, 8br, 8bl, 8/9b, 10tl, 11c, 10./11b, 10/11t, 12c, 12tl, 12/13b, 12/13t, 13br, 15tr, 15bl, 16tl, 16cl, 17tl, 17cr, 17cl, 18b, 19b, 21tl, 24/25c, 26tr, 30/31t. FPG International; 18/19t. Giraudon; 30tl. Images; 2/3t, 25r & OFC (inset pic), 29r. Kobal; 8/9t, 20bl, 24tl, 26c, 26/27. Mary Evans Picture Library; 2cl, 4/5c & 5cr, 8/9b, 10c, 16cr, 16br, 17br, 18bl, 25bl, 27tr. Norio Hayakawa, Groomwatch; 20t. Science Photo Library; IFC, 2tl, 6c, 6/7t & OFC (main pic), 7cr, 18tl, 22/23, 22cb, 22/23cb, 22tl, 22ct, 26l. Telegraph Colour Library; 28/29t. Tony Stone; 20/21c, 29cb.

Every effort has been made to trace the copyright holders and we apologize in advance for any unintentional omissions.

We would be pleased to insert the appropriate acknowledgement in any subsequent edition of this publication.

snapping-turtle
guide